Especially for

....

From

....

Date

....

Latte for Life

Inspiration for Women

BARBOUR
PUBLISHING

Contents

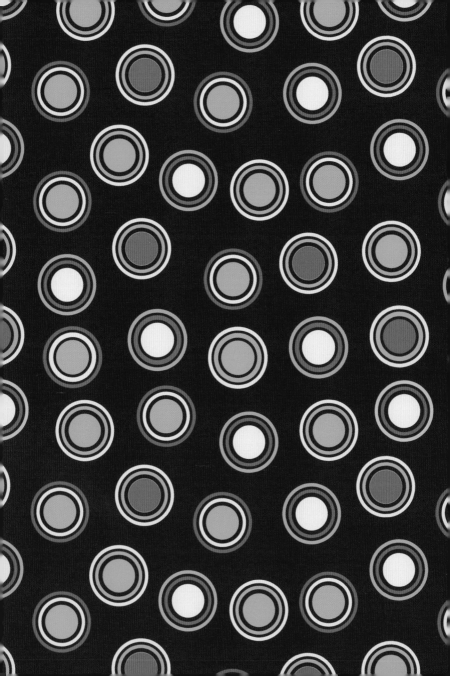

Introduction

Whatever is lovely. . .think about such things.
PHILIPPIANS 4:8 NIV

Help yourself to a little latte for life. . .
and indulge in the spirit-lifting inspiration found
in the pages of this delightful volume. Just-right-
sized readings, along with encouraging thoughts,
quotations, prayers, and scripture—plus delicious ·
latte recipes—will warm your soul.

A little latte for life is just what you need.
Help yourself to a cup!

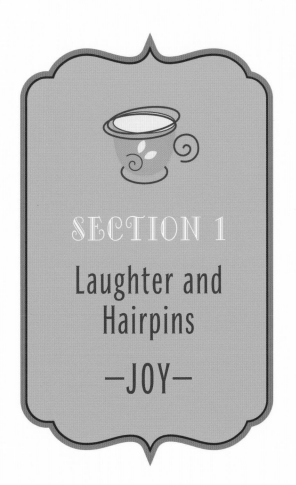

SECTION 1

Laughter and Hairpins

—JOY—

He will yet fill your mouth with laughter and your lips with shouts of joy.

JOB 8:21 NIV

We don't laugh because we're happy—
we're happy because we laugh.

WILLIAM JAMES

$\mathcal{L}$ike most women, I like to look my best when I leave the house. So when I received the worst haircut of my life a few years ago, I was panicked! I had a mullet. To improve my hairstyle during the growing out process, I bought some faux hair that matched my natural hair. It sort of clipped in my natural hair, but it took me awhile to get the hang of it.

Imagine this... I'm in the office of a coworker, discussing the outcome of a meeting we'd just had in the conference room, and as I went over a point very passionately, I flipped my hair. In fact, I flipped it right off my head. My faux hair landed on the ground, near my coworker's feet. She jumped and screamed a bit. (I think she thought it was a gopher or something.) We both laughed until our stomachs hurt.

I learned a valuable lesson that day—well two, actually. First off, it's good to laugh at yourself. And second, always use a lot of bobby pins when securing faux hair.

Laughing together and showing your vulnerability can be very bonding. Don't be afraid to be imperfect with your coworkers and God. They'll love you—mullet and all.

Laughter is the shortest distance between two people.

VICTOR BORGE

A laugh is a smile that bursts.

MARY H. WALDRIP

Laughter Fact:

Laughter should be every woman's favorite exercise. . . For every fabulous belly Laugh, you can burn up to 3.5 calories!

A Latte for Life Moment

Take a break for no reason at all. . .and invite a friend to join you. Sip your favorite coffee drinks, and enjoy good company and great conversation.

I don't have a
problem with caffeine.
I have a problem
without caffeine!

UNKNOWN

Lord, infuse me with life, energy, and joy. I thank You for being my strength and my delight. I don't have to look to a bowl of ice cream or the compliments of a friend to fill me up on the inside. Steady and constant, You are my source; You are the One who fills me. Sustain me, Lord, with the power of Your love, so I can live my life refreshed and renewed.

. . . .

A cheerful heart brings a smile to your face.

PROVERBS 15:13 MSG

Honey-Nut Latte

1 ounce hazelnut syrup
1 ounce honey
1 to 2 ounces espresso
Steamed milk
Whipped topping
Honey to taste
Nuts, finely chopped

In large mug, mix hazelnut syrup and honey with hot espresso; stir until honey dissolves. Fill mug with steamed milk. Garnish with whipped topping, honey, and nuts.

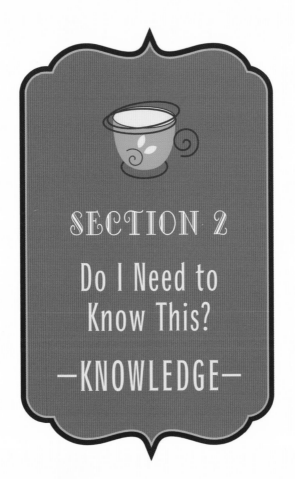

SECTION 2

Do I Need to Know This?

—KNOWLEDGE—

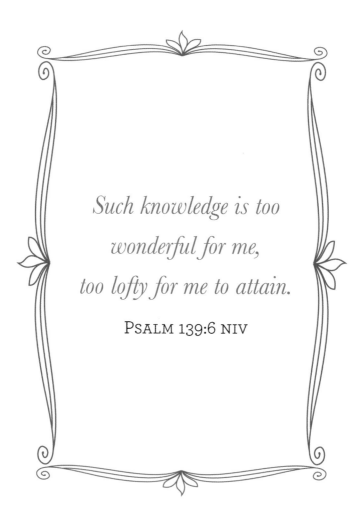

Such knowledge is too wonderful for me, too lofty for me to attain.

PSALM 139:6 NIV

The larger the island of knowledge,
the longer the shoreline of wonder.

RALPH W. SOCKMAN

$\mathcal{I}$ have a theory that the human brain eventually gets full. The tighter you pack it, the more it will leak out old facts, especially as you get older. At least that seems to be my experience. For instance, now that we have grandchildren, it's less important for me to remember my children's names and more important to remember those of my grandchildren, so I have been known to call my son by my grandson's name, or my grandson is suddenly elevated to a son. Something's leaking, you see.

I've become highly selective in what I learn. I fish, but I don't take the fish off the hook. Indeed, the guide gets upset if I even try. It's something I don't need to know right now. I know how to use a computer but choose not to know how to attach files to an e-mail. For now, I get away with it. Would you believe my husband wants me to learn how to balance the checkbook on the computer? I can barely do it with a pencil and handheld calculator!

Where's the blessing in this state of affairs? Well, I've been blessed with a loving family who thinks it's funny when I forget their names. My refusal to learn every silly fact that comes by leaves me with time to play with my grandchildren. I'm sure there's no scientific basis for my "full brain" theory, but it's not a subject I intend to research. It would take up precious room in my brain.

In your thirst for knowledge, be sure not to drown in all the information.

ANTHONY J. D'ANGELO

One part of knowledge consists in being ignorant of such things as are not worthy to be known.

SOCRATES

Knowledge Fact:

Want to improve your ability to
retain knowledge?
Get a good night's sleep!

A Latte for Life Moment

Create some time for daily
spiritual renewal. Relax in
your favorite chair with a
steaming beverage,
your Bible, a devotional,
and a simple treat. Enjoy!

I'd stop drinking lattes, but I'm no quitter.

UNKNOWN

Lord, You have all power and authority. You are the highest ruler in the land— in the entire universe! What a privilege it is to come humbly yet boldly before You and ask You to empower me today. For all I need to do, for all I need to say, may Your favor rest on me. May Your blessings, Lord, flow through my life— and may I also be a blessing to others.

. . . .

Wise people treasure knowledge.

PROVERBS 10:14 NLT

Raspberry Truffle Latte

6 ounces hot brewed coffee
2 tablespoons chocolate syrup
2 tablespoons raspberry syrup
½ cup chocolate ice cream
Whipped topping
Grated chocolate
Fresh raspberries

Mix coffee and flavored syrups in mug.
Spoon ice cream into coffee mixture.
Add whipped topping, grated chocolate,
and fresh raspberries as desired.

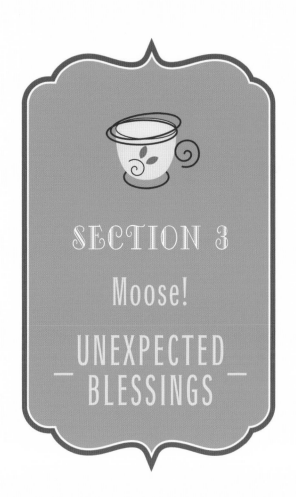

SECTION 3

Moose!

UNEXPECTED
— BLESSINGS —

God made the wild
animals according to their
kinds, the livestock. . .
and all the creatures
that move along the
ground according to
their kinds. And God saw
that it was good.

GENESIS 1:25 NIV

However many blessings we expect from God, His infinite liberality will always exceed all our wishes and our thoughts.

JOHN CALVIN

I know God has a sense of humor. He did, after all, create the moose, which looks like a horse gone incredibly wrong. I met my first moose in the middle of an isolated logging road. We made the mistake of rounding a blind bend a little too fast, coming face-to-knee with a young animal who stood his ground in true moose fashion. My first thought was, *He's so big!* Television or photographs do not convey the sheer massiveness of a moose—even a young one.

Moose are not overly intelligent. Fortunately, they are exceedingly calm, collected animals, curious and patient with humans who invade their space. They look us over and usually decide we're no threat—not a wise decision during hunting season. This particular moose blocked the road for a good ten minutes to look us over before ambling off into the bushes on moose business.

No human who has ever shared space with a moose can avoid loving them. Their ugliness, their bony legs, their cowlike eyes—you just can't resist them, even though you know they can do fatal damage if they collide with a car. They are somewhat like an ugly baby—always a surprise, but one that makes you smile in spite of yourself and thank God for providing such an unexpected delight. God didn't make the moose beautiful or smart, just irresistible, and seeing a moose can only be a blessing.

In order to attract more of the blessings that life has to offer, you must truly appreciate what you already have.

RALPH MARSTON

Our prayers should be for blessings in general, for God knows best what is good for us.

SOCRATES

Blessings Fact:

A man may lose the good things of this life against his will; but if he loses the eternal blessings, he does so with his own consent.

AUGUSTINE

A Latte for Life Moment

The best time of day for a latte is...

      Breakfast, for a jumpstart to your day.

      Midmorning, for a little inspiration.

      Lunch, for good measure.

      Midafternoon, for a restart to your day.

      Dinner, for a conversation starter.

      Evening, to end the day right!

A little of what you fancy does you good.

MARIE LLOYD

Father God, Your hands created the heavens and the earth. You breathed upon Adam and gave him life. Everything that was created was created through Your Son Jesus Christ. The trees, the earth, the waters, and the creatures clap their hands in praise to You. This is the day that You have made! I will rejoice and be glad in it as I shout Your name to the heavens!

. . . .

My cup overflows with blessings.

PSALM 23:5 NLT

Pumpkin Spice Latte

1 shot (1 to 1.5 ounces) brewed espresso
2 tablespoons canned pumpkin puree
1 teaspoon vanilla extract
2 tablespoons white sugar
¼ teaspoon pumpkin pie spice
1 cup milk

While preparing espresso, whisk together
pumpkin, vanilla, sugar, pumpkin pie spice,
and milk in small saucepan over medium
heat. Stir constantly until hot and frothy.
Do not boil. Pour espresso into mug and
top off with pumpkin mixture.

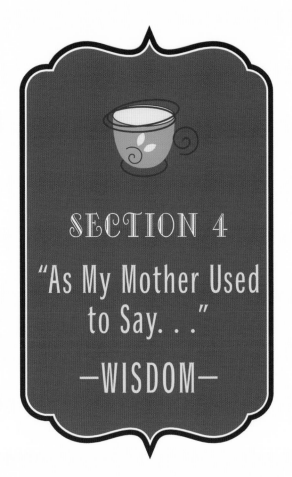

SECTION 4

"As My Mother Used to Say..."

—WISDOM—

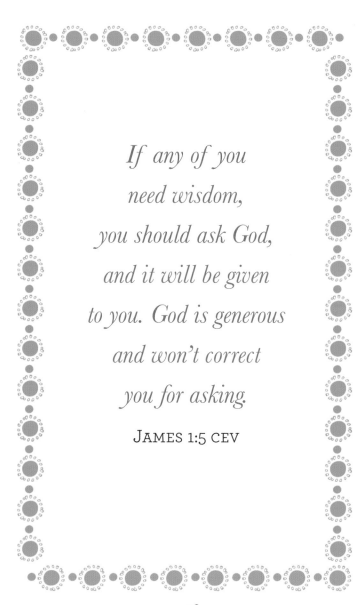

If any of you
need wisdom,
you should ask God,
and it will be given
to you. God is generous
and won't correct
you for asking.

JAMES 1:5 CEV

Wisdom is the reward you get for a lifetime of listening when you'd have preferred to talk.

DOUG LARSON

The older I've gotten, the more I've heard myself uttering the words, "Well, as my mother used to say. . ." It's almost become a joke among my friends, and they'll start to grin even before I can get some pithy proverb out. In fact, some of my mother's sayings are quite humorous, filled with homespun advice and earthy metaphors, like the day she was canning some beans and told me she was "hotter than a tent preacher in July." We're from Alabama, and I can assure you that camp meetings in the summer can get pretty hot!

It's not just the down-to-earth proverbs, however, that I depend on. My mother's wisdom sometimes amazes me. I began to ask her advice on people and situations when I was still just a kid, and she has seldom steered me wrong. When a kid was trying to bully me in junior high school, her advice helped me ease the situation in just a few days. When dealing with a variety of men in college had me spinning in confusion, she helped me find my feet again. She taught me how to handle work, money, even my faith.

I once asked her about the source of her wisdom, and she responded, "A little bit of living and a whole lot of prayer."

My mother had learned to rely on God for her guidance and inspiration, which had made her invaluable to her friends and family. Even the tiniest problems were turned over to God, which gave her the confidence to help out those who came to her for advice.

I think it's very revealing that wisdom in scripture is portrayed as a woman (see Proverbs 1:20–21), since women seem to have an instinctual sense of how to take the little lessons of life and scripture and use them to nurture those they love. Even more encouraging is this reminder from James, that if we ever think we're lacking in wisdom, all we have to do is ask—and God will provide both wisdom and the confidence to use it.

**There is a wisdom of the head, and. . .
a wisdom of the heart.**

CHARLES DICKENS

*Wisdom is oftentimes nearer when
we stoop than when we soar.*

WILLIAM WORDSWORTH

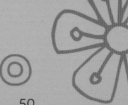

Wisdom Fact:

Joyful is the person who finds wisdom.

PROVERBS 3:13 NLT

A Latte for Life Moment

A good way to show love
to a friend: a steaming
latte and quality time with
wonderful you!

Can one desire too much of a good thing?

WILLIAM SHAKESPEARE

Lord, I want to be a woman of wisdom, not foolishness. Help me to make right choices and conduct myself in a manner worthy of Your name. I pray that I would be honest and upright in my daily life so my actions reflect who You are. Help me to act with integrity, so I become a person who keeps her promises and commitments.

. . . .

For wisdom will enter your heart,
and knowledge will fill you with joy.

PROVERBS 2:10 NLT

Caramel Latte

1 tablespoon brown sugar
¼ cup half-and-half
¾ cup hot, brewed coffee
1 tablespoon caramel ice cream topping

Stir brown sugar into half-and-half until dissolved. Whip with small whisk. Pour coffee into mug, and stir in caramel sauce until dissolved. Pour half-and-half/brown sugar mixture into coffee and serve.

SECTION 5
Sweet Dreams
—WORRIES—

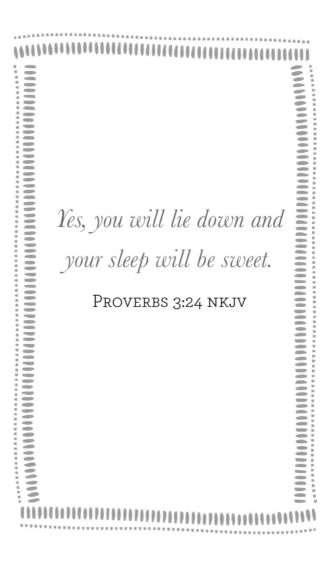

Yes, you will lie down and your sleep will be sweet.

PROVERBS 3:24 NKJV

Worry never robs tomorrow of its sorrow, it only saps today of its joy.

LEO BUSCAGLIA

59

Okay, I admit it. I am a worrier. I don't intentionally worry. In fact, my worrying usually starts as wondering, which leads to reasoning, which leads to worrying, which almost always leads to sleepless nights. Ever been there?

You're lying in bed. The lights are off. Everyone else, including the dog, is asleep, but you can't turn off your mind. Your brain continues to crank, trying to figure out how to solve some crisis at work. Slowly, the tension headache begins, creeping up your neck and spreading over your entire head. That's it. Now you're wide awake and in pain. So you watch reruns on TV as the clock ticks into the wee hours of the night.

I have spent more nights living out that scenario than I'd like to admit. But you know what? Worrying about the problems at work never changed a single one of them. Now if I happen to have a restless night, I spend it in prayer. I thank God for watching over me. I thank Him for wisdom. I thank Him for favor with my boss. And I fall asleep in peace— no headaches, no worries. God promises us sweet slumber in Proverbs, so hold Him to it. Sweet dreams, sister!

That the birds of worry and care fly over your head, this you cannot change, but that they build nests in your hair, this you can prevent.

CHINESE PROVERB

I have learned to live each day as it comes, and not to borrow trouble by dreading tomorrow.

DOROTHY DIX

Worry Fact:

The most perfect way to conquer worry is through prayer!

A Latte for Life Moment

In nearly every crisis,
whether great or imagined,
there's nothing that a little
latte can't cure!

Latte and laughter:
two of life's sweetest gifts!

Lord, I don't want to be anxious about anything, but so often I am. I thank You that You understand. Right now I release my burdens and cares to You. I give You my heavy heart and my flailing emotions. I ask that You calm me, despite all that is happening in my life. As I keep my thoughts, actions, and attitudes centered on Jesus, Your peace comes. I thank You for Your peace that settles on me even when I do not understand.

• •

"Can all your worries add a single moment to your life?"

MATTHEW 6:27 NLT

Gingerbread Latte

2 ounces espresso
2 tablespoons gingerbread flavored syrup
½ cup steamed milk
⅛ cup whipped cream
1 pinch ground cinnamon
1 pinch ground nutmeg
½ teaspoon vanilla powder

In coffee mug, combine espresso with syrup.
Pour in steamed milk. Top with whipped
cream then sprinkle with cinnamon,
nutmeg, and vanilla powder. Serve.

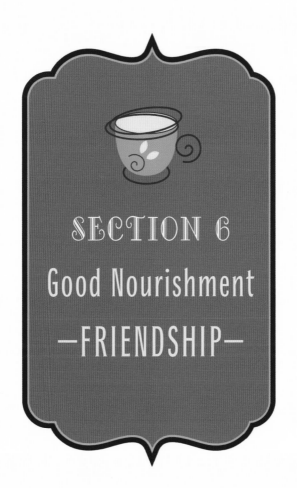

SECTION 6
Good Nourishment
—FRIENDSHIP—

A sweet friendship

refreshes the soul.

PROVERBS 27:9 MSG

A friend is a present you give to yourself.

ROBERT LOUIS STEVENSON

No one seems to have time for friendship these days. Everyone is overscheduled, and if there's one thing friendship requires, it's time. You have to invite prospective friends over for an evening before you even know whether they are prospective friends. If you seem compatible, you have to keep investing time to allow a friendship to blossom. Finding a friend is as challenging as finding a spouse.

There are also various levels of friendship to consider. Casual friendships are easy: They are pleasant to spend an evening with, go to weekend events with, and catch up on local gossip with. But these are superficial friendships and soon die if someone moves away or their children transfer to a different school. They're like a nice dessert, but they aren't very enriching.

Then there are serious friendships that can endure anything, forgive everything. These are few and hard to find. They may grow from casual friendships but most likely do not because of the huge investment they require. Once acquired, friends like these are precious blessings. You can call these friends at 3 a.m., and they will be there for you. In times of tragedy, they will listen to you cry and cry with you. In good times, you will want to share your joy with them, and your happiness will make them happy. Good friends are good nourishment for the heart and soul. Take the time needed to build such friendships, and you will never be lonely again.

The greatest sweetener of human life is friendship.

JOSEPH ADDISON

A loyal friend laughs at your jokes
when they're not so good
and sympathizes with your problems
when they're not so bad.

ARNOLD H. GLASGOW

Friendship Fact:

Friendships not only make you happier, but they can make you healthier, too! Creating strong bonds with another person helps lower blood pressure, heart rate, and cholesterol.

A Latte for Life Moment

Take time in your day to
be inspired by something
small—the scent of a flower,
a hug from a child, lattes and
conversation shared with a
friend. . . Then thank God for
the little things in life.

Whenever you are sincerely pleased, you are nourished.

RALPH WALDO EMERSON

Lord, help me to be a friend who loves at all times, even when I may not feel like it. Teach me how to love with words—to be encouraging and supportive—and help me to show love by my actions, too. I want to be a better listener, never self-centered. Show me how to bring joy to others in tangible ways, with a phone call, a hug, or a deed that is meaningful to my friends.

. . . .

The seeds of good deeds become a tree of life;
a wise person wins friends.

PROVERBS 11:30 NLT

Frozen Latte for Two

¾ cup cold water
¾ cup milk
2 tablespoons instant coffee granules
1 cup ice cubes
2 tablespoons sugar, or more to taste

Add water, milk, and coffee to blender; cover. Blend mixture until coffee granules are dissolved. Add ice and sugar; blend until smooth. Serve immediately.

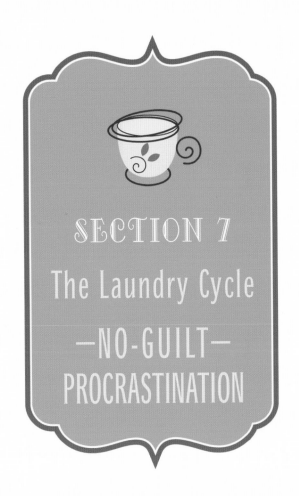

SECTION 7

The Laundry Cycle

—NO-GUILT—
PROCRASTINATION

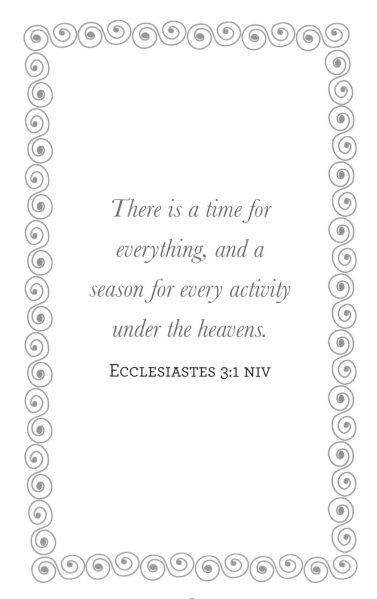

There is a time for everything, and a season for every activity under the heavens.

ECCLESIASTES 3:1 NIV

One of the greatest labor-saving inventions
of today is tomorrow.

VINCENT T. FOSS

In our house, a piece of laundry takes about four days from start to finish. The first day it's run through the washer and dryer. The second, it sits in the dryer developing the proper number of wrinkles. The third day I reheat and fold it. The fourth day it's put away. That's assuming I haven't run out of something vital or created a roadblock by washing more than one load a day, in which case folded laundry piles up, and the cats sleep on it, requiring a second run through the washer and dryer.

I don't normally procrastinate in life's little chores. Papers never pile up on my desk. I have a mental to-do list and enjoy working my way through it, but somehow laundry always sinks to the bottom of my list. We adapt. I can wear a pair of jeans for two days if necessary. My husband has discovered he can wear swimming trunks under his business suit when all else fails, since he would not think of buying a week's worth of anything at once.

Things are not going to change, laundry-wise. Now that the kids are gone, so is my motivation. Not doing laundry frees up time to read a book, visit the grandchildren, go fishing, or even take a nap. I love laundry simply because I can always put it off for another day without guilt.

Never put off until tomorrow what you can do the day after tomorrow.

Mark Twain

The key is not to prioritize what's on your schedule, but to schedule your priorities.

Stephen R. Covey

Guilt-Free Fact:

Research has proven that dark chocolate reduces stress hormones. So. . .the laundry can wait until tomorrow. Grab a bar of chocolate and relax awhile!

A Latte for Life Moment

Do you find that you spend
too much time worrying about
what you just *have* to get done?
Intentionally redirect your
thoughts toward gratitude.
What are you most thankful for?
Your health? A loving family? A
great career? You'll quickly forget
about your worries when you see
how richly the Lord has blessed you.

A friend in need. . .
is a friend in need of a latte!

Quiet my soul, Lord. Help me to lay my worries and stresses at Your feet and focus on enjoying time with my family. Remind me that it's okay to cut out the unnecessary tasks today and to leave some things for tomorrow. Amen.

• •

"Be still, and know that I am God."

PSALM 46:10 NIV

Crème Brûlée Latte

2 tablespoons caramel topping, divided
1 ounce vanilla syrup
2 ounces espresso or strong coffee
8 ounces steamed milk

Lace sides of coffee mug with 1 tablespoon caramel topping. Then place vanilla syrup at the bottom of cup and top with espresso or coffee. Heat milk by steaming it using an espresso machine or by slowly heating it over medium heat then whipping it until desired amount of froth is created. Fill cup with steamed milk and top with remaining caramel.

SECTION 8

No Limits!

—CONFIDENCE—

The Spirit itself beareth witness with our spirit, that we are the children of God: And if children, then heirs; heirs of God, and joint-heirs with Christ.

ROMANS 8:16–17 KJV

Always act like you're
wearing an invisible crown.

UNKNOWN

When you look in the mirror, what do you see? Do you see a woman who is smart and talented, or do you see a woman who never quite measures up? Often the limitations that we place on ourselves have nothing to do with who we really are or the strengths God has given us. They're more about how we see ourselves. Even if the rest of the world sees us as confident, smart women, we can limit ourselves by our own view.

If you're limiting your success and peace of mind because of how you see yourself, begin to immerse yourself in God's Word. If necessary, talk to a pastor or counselor. God doesn't want you to live with the heaviness of never thinking you're good enough. If you are a child of God then you are more than good enough. You are His heir and a joint-heir with Jesus. Through the sacrifice of Jesus Christ, you are good enough—regardless of what others say or have said, regardless of what you've ever done. If you don't believe me, just ask your heavenly Father.

If we all did the things we are
capable of doing, we would literally
astound ourselves.

THOMAS ALVA EDISON

The best way to gain
self-confidence is to do what you
are afraid to do.

UNKNOWN

Confidence Fact:

Women and men who are 70 to 90 percent self-assured are among the happiest and most successful people.

A Latte for Life Moment

The more one does and sees and
feels, the more one is able to do,
and the more genuine may be one's
appreciation of fundamental things
like home, and love,
and understanding companionship.

AMELIA EARHART

The most wasted of all days is
one without a latte — (or two)!

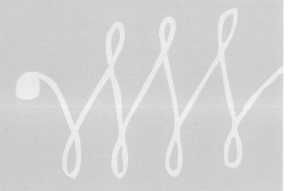

Lord, I want to be a more confident woman. I don't want to be afraid of disasters—or just making mistakes. Give me the courage to know that You, Lord, will be my confidence.

You keep me from tripping over my tongue and saying the wrong thing. But even when I do, You have the power to make things right again. Thank You for the confidence You give me. Let me walk with my head high because I know who I am in Christ: I am Yours!

. . . .

The Lord will be at your side and will keep your foot from being snared.

PROVERBS 3:26 NIV

Chocolate Mint Latte

¾ ounce chocolate mint syrup
1 to 2 shots espresso
Steamed milk

Pour flavored syrup into coffee mug.
Add espresso—one to two shots, depending
on your taste. Stir. Top with foamy,
steamed milk. Serve.

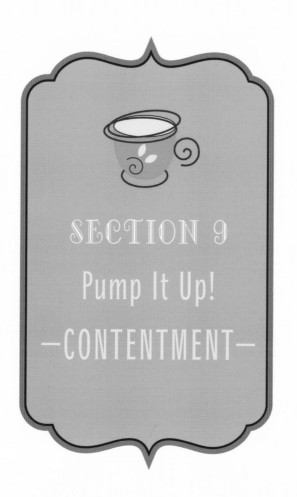

SECTION 9
Pump It Up!
—CONTENTMENT—

*Through Him, therefore,
let us constantly and at all
times offer up to God
a sacrifice of praise,
which is the fruit of
lips that thankfully
acknowledge and confess
and glorify His name.*

HEBREWS 13:15 AMP

Seeing our Father in everything makes life one long thanksgiving and gives rest to the heart.

HANNAH WHITALL SMITH

*B*e honest. . .you were feeling pretty content in your job and your overall life until you ran into *her*. She drove up in her new Cadillac Escalade, pulled in next to you, and shared how she'd just been hired to a new position that pays three times what you currently make. And to top it off, she just lost fourteen pounds on the South Beach Diet. Suddenly, all of your contentment vanished. Instead, that contentment was replaced with resentment, envy, and a little bit of anger.

If you've ever experienced a situation similar to this one, you know how miserable it can make you. It can totally rob you of your joy. There's only one way to fight off the resentment and envy that follow an encounter like the one described above. You have to pump up the praise. That's right—praise the Lord like you've never praised before. Don't dwell on what you don't have. Meditate on what you do have. Praise God for the good things in your life. And praise Him for the blessings in your friend's life, too. Praise will bring peace and contentment to your heart, and it's a lot more fun than the South Beach Diet.

And I smiled to think God's greatness
flowed around our incompleteness,
round our restlessness, His rest.

ELIZABETH BARRETT BROWNING

Sweet are the thoughts that savor
of content. The quiet mind is
richer than a crown.

ROBERT GREENE

Contentment Fact:

Yet true godliness with contentment
is itself great wealth.

1 Timothy 6:6 nlt

A Latte for Life Moment

Make the conscious choice to be content with your life. You'll be delighted at what a change this simple but powerful choice will make in your life!

Ponder well on this point:
The pleasant hours of our life
are all connected by a more
or less tangible link with some
memory of the table.

CHARLES PIERRE MONSELET

Lord, please help me to find my contentment in You. I don't want to be defined by "stuff"—the things I own or what I do. May my greatest happiness in life be knowing who You are and who I am in Christ. May I treasure the simple things in life, those things that bring me peace. With Your grace I rest secure. You, Lord, are my satisfaction.

. . . .

The mind governed by the Spirit is life and peace.

ROMANS 8:6 NIV

Chai Latte

1 cup milk
1 cup water
1 strip orange peel
3 whole cloves
1 (2 inch) cinnamon stick
3 whole black peppercorns
1 pinch ground nutmeg
4 teaspoons sugar
2 teaspoons black tea leaves

Combine milk and water in saucepan over medium-high heat. Once mixture has warmed, add orange peel, cloves, cinnamon stick, peppercorns, nutmeg, sugar, and tea leaves. Bring to a boil then reduce heat and simmer until color deepens. Strain out spices, and pour into cups. Serve.

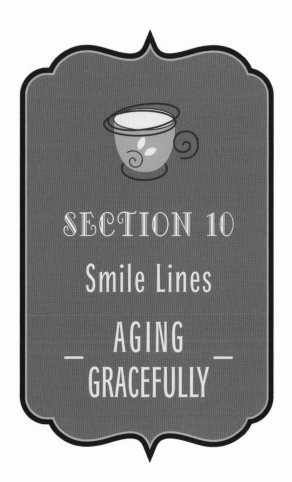

SECTION 10

Smile Lines

AGING GRACEFULLY

He has made everything beautiful in its time.

ECCLESIASTES 3:11 NIV

Wrinkles should merely indicate where smiles have been.

Mark Twain

Some cosmetics company sent me a sample container of anti-wrinkle face cream to try out, claiming I would see a difference before the container was empty. They were right, but not in the way they anticipated. I tried it for a few days then gave my face a good look under a strong light. Big mistake. I saw every wrinkle, ding, and flaw I have accumulated in sixty-three years—wrinkles I'd never even suspected were there until the magic cream arrived.

I'm still in shock. I don't know whether the cream helped or not because I'd never noticed my face's destruction before and can't make an intelligent comparison. All I know is that my mother's skin now rules my face.

The funny thing is, I don't really remember my mother's skin as being wrinkled. She had freckles that appeared if she stayed in the sun too long, and she burned easily, being a redhead. I remember her dark, kind eyes and her perpetual smile, and I suppose she had her fair share of what she would call smile lines, but in my mind's eye she is totally without flaw.

I hope my children's memories of me will overlook my flaws, too. In the meantime, I'll use up my sample. It was free, and it taught me some very nice lessons on the art of aging gracefully.

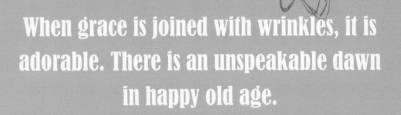

When grace is joined with wrinkles, it is adorable. There is an unspeakable dawn in happy old age.

VICTOR HUGO

The great thing about getting older is that you don't lose all the other ages you've been.

MADELEINE L'ENGLE

Fun Aging Fact:

Two body parts never stop growing from birth—your nose and your ears.

A Latte for Life Moment

Invite a friend over for coffee or tea. You'll find that the conversation and company will lift your spirit and rejuvenate your soul.

Sleep is a symptom of caffeine deprivation.

UNKNOWN

Lord, our world is so focused on outward appearance—nice clothes and good looks. But You're never like that. People may look at the hairstyles and outfits, but You look at the heart. Lord, please help me to work with what You've given me on the outside—as I also polish my inner character. May Your beauty shine through me as I praise You more and more. Be my light within that I may radiate the love of Christ.

. . . .

"The LORD does not look at things people look at. People look at the outward appearance, but the LORD looks at the heart."

1 SAMUEL 16:7 NIV

Triple Berry Latte

½ ounce blueberry syrup
½ ounce strawberry syrup
½ ounce raspberry syrup
2 shots espresso
Steamed milk

Pour syrup into mug. Add espresso and
swirl to mix. Top with steamed milk. Serve.